Theophilus Stork

Luther at Home

Theophilus Stork

Luther at Home

ISBN/EAN: 9783337127169

Printed in Europe, USA, Canada, Australia, Japan

Cover: Foto ©Lupo / pixelio.de

More available books at **www.hansebooks.com**

LUTHER AT HOME.

DR. STORK'S WRITINGS.

HOME-SCENES OF THE NEW TESTAMENT.

GELZER'S LIFE OF LUTHER.
        Edited, with an Introduction.

CHILDREN OF THE NEW TESTAMENT.

LUTHER'S CHRISTMAS-TREE.

JESUS IN THE TEMPLE.

THE UNSEEN WORLD.

LUTHER AT HOME.

LUTHER'S MARRIAGE.

Luther at Home.

BY

T. STORK, D. D.

PHILADELPHIA:
LUTHERAN BOARD OF PUBLICATION.
1872.

Entered, according to Act of Congress, in the year 1871, by
LUTHERAN BOARD OF PUBLICATION,
in the Office of the Librarian of Congress, at Washington.

STEREOTYPED BY J. FAGAN & SON, PHILADELPHIA.

CAXTON PRESS OF SHERMAN & CO.

PREFACE

THESE pen and picture sketches are designed to familiarize the young with the most beautiful and instructive aspects and incidents of Luther's home-life. It is hoped, morever, that this portraiture of the great Reformer, as he appears in the privacy of home, will serve, in some measure, to counteract the tendency to individualism in our day, and to expose the vandalism that would substitute the freedom of affinities for the sacred bonds of matrimony, and break the wedding-ring as a superstitious symbol.

No doubt there are inhumanities sheltered under the very sacredness of the domestic relations; but everything has its shadow, and evils mingle with all human relations, and there are sometimes grievous wrongs and oppressions perpetrated under the very sanctity of the home-life. But surely we are not, on this account, to break the sacred bonds of the marriage relation, and set the family group adrift in some vague conceit of social freedom or some nonsense of spiritual affinities: this would be like knocking a ship to pieces because some of the passengers are sea-sick. "This organism of the family *is* a ship that has carried human civilization over the waves of ages — an ark that has preserved the germs of the social state in many a deluge. Sunder the ties that hold it together, and who can estimate the ruin, or from the shattered fragments reconstruct society?"

The example of Luther may also suggest and practically illustrate what a beauty and blessedness belong to a truly Christian domestic life. How much there is to love and to enjoy in a true home; and what divergent lines of destiny reach out from the cradle to immortal issues.

And then it may suggest, to all who are married, the importance of having a home. There may be, to some, a necessity of boarding. But where such a sort of living is matter of choice from a love of ease or luxury, of fashion or a morbid fondness for society, then it cannot be too strongly deprecated. Better, it seems to us, that the family should live in a shanty, which they can call their own home, than in the stateliest mansion open to everybody; which is like lodging on the house-top and eating in the street. Especially does tender childhood need the dews of domestic influences, and cannot unfold sweetly and naturally in the gairish sunlight and the rude contacts of the roadside.

There is yet another thing suggested in this home-life of Luther, and that is, that every family needs the love and care of a father's heart. With all that a mother may do, the home that does not feel a father's loving sympathy is *not* a home. No man can have such grand enterprises, and such cares and toils, as absorbed the thoughts and busied the hands of Luther. And yet he found time and a heart for the pleasures and enjoyments of domestic life. No man has a right to let his entire heart melt away in business, and carry none of it home with him. There never was a business interest yet that ought to put out the light on the hearth-stone, or disarm a father, in the midst of his children, of kindness, cheerfulness, hope, and faith.

We trust this humble effort to portray the home-life of the great Reformer may, at least, awaken the inquiry in every reader: "What is home to *me?*" And as you follow Luther as he appears in these pen pictures and home scenes, will you allow and ponder the questions: "Is home a place of serious thought as well as of love and gladness? Have you an altar of prayer there? Is it overarched by the presence of God, and brightened by His benediction? Do you comprehend the meaning of the communions that are brightened by its fire-light, of the shadowy memories that fresco its walls? Is it a little thing to you that the cry of birth has been heard beneath its roof, that the mystery of death has descended into its chambers? Is there no solemnity as well as gladness in the relations of husband and wife, of father and mother—a solemnity that links time to eternity, and earth with heaven? Is not home full of incentives, full of voices calling to duty and love, to faith and prayer?"

Contents

	PAGE
THE HOME-LIFE OF MARTIN LUTHER.	13
MARRIAGE.	27
SINGING WITH HIS FAMILY.	47
SUMMER JOYS WITH HIS FAMILY.	85
WINTER PLEASURES.	111
HOME IN SORROW.	133

THE HOME-LIFE

OF

MARTIN LUTHER.

THE

HOME-LIFE

OF

MARTIN LUTHER.

NO man since the time of Paul has occupied so much of human thought, or so lived in the grateful memory of the Christian world, as Martin Luther. His eventful life of noble words and heroic deeds is the grandest fact of modern history. His confession of the true faith is still shaping the religious sentiment of the evangelical Church; and his ideal of personal liberty is still felt in every pulse of human freedom and every step of Christian civilization.

No eulogy of marble or of song can adequately celebrate the greatness of his work for the Church and the world.

> "Nothing can cover his high fame but Heaven;
> No monument set off his memories
> But the eternal substance of his greatness."

Ours is an humbler and all the more grateful, and perhaps needful, task of portraying Luther's domestic life.

The stern and unique grandeur of his public life only makes one the more curious to see how that life looks in the privacy of home; for the household is the home of the man as well as of the child. And what the man is there, is not only a truer revelation of himself, but it is nearer and dearer to us than any public events of his life which make his fame and attract the admiration of the world. The events of domestic life are in the line and sympathy of our own living. What are called public events may or may not be ours in any sense of a common thought or feeling. Hence the home-life of great men has always a peculiar and universal interest. And for the same reason *The Cotter's Saturday Night* has about it such a charm, simply because it is so human, and touches in us so many home feelings and memories.

We can have no true idea of Luther, as a man, apart from his home-life. In the flush and excitement of his public career, he is the creature of passion and impulse, and moves in a sort of artificial light, so that he is seen in that elusive and mystic haze of glory that excludes any true vision and estimate of the man. It is only when he is out of this fictitious glare of public life, and in the quiet, unaffected habitudes of home, with his wife and children, that we see him as he really is.

It is said that a man of letters is often a man of two natures, — the one a book nature, the other a human nature, — and the two are sometimes in painful antagonism. Hence we hear so much of the infelicities of great men in their domestic life. And when one reads of the unhappy homes of Molière and Rousseau, and the ungenial firesides of such men as Dante, Milton, Addison, and Steele, and even of the sainted Hooker, it might well make us timid in lifting the veil from the home of the immortal Reformer, lest some infelicities of his private life should dim the glory of his public career. But, on the other hand, some of the sweetest pictures of human life are found among those which represent the homes of great men who married happily. And among all the honored homes of history, there is none more genial and happy than that of the great Reformer.

Looking at Luther as he appeared in public, and prior to any knowledge of his private life, we might come to a very different conclusion. Seeing him as he appears in exciting controversy, when his very words were battles, and in his fulminations against a rotten priesthood and a despotic hierarchy, or with his stern look and defiant attitude before the Diet of Worms, we might take him for a man with a heart of stone and nerves of steel. And yet such an inference would be as unsound in theory as we happily know it is false in fact. "True greatness," says Lavater, "is always simple and tender." Homer, the matchless painter of men, represents Ajax, the bravest, and Ulysses, the wisest, as often weeping. And Luther, whose heroic deeds shook the very foundations of the mightiest kingdom, was as gentle and loving in his social life as a little child.

Carlyle, with his keen, philosophic eye, seems to see this blending of the hero and the child, the fearless daring and winsome gentleness, in the very face and physique of the great Reformer. He says: "Luther's face is to me expressive of him: in Cranach's best portraits I find the true Luther. A rude, plebeian face, with its huge crag-like brows and bones, the emblem of rugged energy; at first almost a repulsive face. Yet in the eyes especially there is a wild, silent sorrow — an unnamable melancholy, the element of all gentle and fine affections — giving to the rest the true stamp of nobleness." And then in his peculiar style and imagery he goes on to give his own portraiture of Luther in a few bold outlines and exquisite touches. "I will call this Luther a true Great Man; great in intellect, in courage, affection, and integrity; one of our most lovable and precious men. Great, not as a hewn obelisk, but as an Alpine mountain — so simple, honest, spontaneous, not setting up to be great at all; there for quite another purpose than being great! Ah, yes, unsubduable granite, piercing far and wide into the heavens; yet in the cleft of it, fountains, green, beautiful valleys, with flowers!" Again, he says: "A most gentle heart withal, full of pity and love, as indeed the truly valiant heart ever is. I know few things more touching than those soft breathings of affection, soft as a child's or mother's, in this great wild heart of Luther."

This is substantially the view of Luther given by Heine, the pensive but brilliant poet of Germany: "Then he had qualities which are seldom found united, which we are accustomed to regard as irreconcilable antagonisms. He was at the same time a dreamy mystic and a practical man of action. . . . When he had plagued himself all day long with his doctrinal distinctions, in the evening he took his flute, and gazed at the stars, dissolved in melody and devotion. He could be soft as a tender maiden. Sometimes he was wild as the storm that uproots the oak, and then again he was gentle as the zephyr that dallies with the violet."

Perhaps the truest as well as the most comprehensive of all portraitures of Luther is that of Melancthon, in which he says that Luther's character is delineated in those words of St. Paul: "Whatsover things are true, whatsoever things are honest, whatsoever things are just, whatsoever things are pure, whatsoever things are lovely, whatsoever things are of good report."

And yet comparatively few seem to understand *"whatsoever things are lovely"* in Luther's character. A short time since a distinguished minister affirmed in his pulpit that Luther was too sombre and one-sided. That he was a great man, and had done great things for the Church, but that he was altogether too sober and narrow, and lacked the genial mirth and sunny side of a full and rounded manhood. This was a total misconception of the Reformer. For of all distinguished men absorbed in great ideas of reform, and intent upon their accomplishment, Luther was the most genial and sunny in his private life. He was many-sided, and touched all life with a quick and responsive sympathy peculiar to himself.

If it be true that "the child is father of the man," then there must be in the true man something of the child-nature. The childhood, in its loves and fancies and sympathies, must live on in the true *manhood* of the man. And so it appears pre-eminently in Luther. He had all the simplicity of a child in his love of nature and flowers and music. This phase of his life will come out more fully as we proceed to look at Luther in his family. For it is when great men are free from the affectations and conventionalisms that belong to public life, that they appear in their true and simple manhood; for there

> "The man is never in his name absorbed,—
> Chained like a captive to his own renown."

Such a man was fitted alike for the great deeds of the Reformation and the quiet pleasures of social and domestic life. He could pass gracefully from the gaze and admiration of the multitude to sport with his children as he had sported with crowns, and to cultivate his little garden at Wittenberg with the same earnestness he had employed to convert Eck or Zwingle. In the language of Audin, the brilliant French Romanist: "It must be a curious chapter in the history of the human heart to behold the quiet occupations of this monk, whom Charles V. was not able to subdue, who dared to insult Henry VIII., and whose obstinacy Leo X., Adrian, and Clement had not been able to overcome;—but who, in the midst of his family, seemed to have lost all recollection of his past glory, and was willing to be concealed from the world that he might enjoy the delights of love and friendship, and give to the world the example of the domestic virtues which Plutarch so much loved to describe."

MARRIAGE.

MARRIAGE.

"A husband in the great Reformer see,
Like Martin Luther, and like nothing more!
. . . .
Looks he less lofty to those hearts which love
The sterling and the true, when playful seen
In the mild sunshine of a married state?"

THE Reformer's true home life began with his marriage. To this important step he was prompted, not so much from natural inclination, as from the urgent wishes of his aged father and his own personal convictions of duty. He believed that he was called to the marriage state not only as a man, but as a reformer. The enforcement of celibacy on the clergy was, in his now enlightened views, not only wrong in itself, but productive of enormous immorality. His study of the Bible, as well as his knowledge of the impurity of the religious orders for centuries, led him to regard marriage as the natural and healthy state in which clergy as well as laity were intended to live. It was the condition in which humanity was at once purest and happiest.

It was with such views he determined to marry. He said: "We may be able to live unmarried; but in these days we must protest in deed as well as in word against the doctrine of celibacy. It is an invention of Satan." His friend Schurff, the lawyer, said: "If this monk should marry, he will make all the world and the devil himself burst with laughter, and will destroy the work so grandly begun." This sarcasm only strengthened Luther in his purpose, and boldly raising his head, he exclaimed: "Well, then, I will do it; I will play the devil and the world this trick; I will content my father and marry Catharine."

Catharine von Bora, whom he chose for his wife, was a nun of good family, left homeless by the breaking up of her convent. How it happened that Luther and Catharine came together is happily told by "E. B. S.," in the Lutheran Home Journal of 1853:

"A tenant of the convent of Nimptisch, in Saxony, she was snatched as it were from a living death by the writings of the great Reformer, whose works were read by the nuns of this cloister by permission of the Lady Abbess, with the pious design of arousing in their minds an abhorrence of the wicked heretic Luther. But the beautiful Ketha, with eight of her companions, arose from their perusal and study to bless

Luther, who brought to them the joyful news of a free and full salvation. They all fled from the convent, and Ketha found protection and a refuge with the Burgomaster of Wittenberg, and also with Philip and Margaret Melancthon. While sojourning with her truly Christian friends, the lovely Catharine had several distinguished suitors for the honor of her hand, but she requested of her friend Margaret that she might not be persecuted with their undesired attentions, as her heart could never be interested in any of them; and with a true woman's tact, Margaret perfectly understood her friend, whom she not a little annoyed by her playful pleasantries concerning the 'terrible Luther's' monkish notions. For, although not approving of the celibacy of the monks and clergy, he had, it seems, considered the question settled that *he* was *not* to marry. At this time he must have been about forty years old, and Margaret intuitively perceived that the young Ketha's enthusiastic veneration for her unseen liberator possessed the germs of an incipient, yet faithful and blessed attachment. It was rather a curious circumstance, that of Luther's being employed by Catharine's most persevering admirer to plead for him, and secure an interest in the heart of the reluctant fair one. He undertook the matter, supposing that some religious scruples were in the way, and he was not a little surprised and puzzled at Catharine's continued inflexibility. But

' The bard has sung, God never formed a soul
    Without its own peculiar mate, to meet
 Its wandering half, when ripe to crown the whole
    Bright plan of bliss, most heavenly, most complete!'

And thus was the surprised and grateful Luther led to his Ketha, the crowning star of his eventful life of toil and labor."

In the beautiful month of June, 1525, in a private chapel of the house of the Registrar of Wittenberg, Luther was married to Catharine von Bora. As represented in Kœnig's picture, "the jurist, Apel, and the great painter, Cranach, stand on either side; Bugenhagen blesses the plighted troth of Luther and Catharine, who kneel before him, she with her long hair flowing over her shoulders, and the marriage-wreath on her brow, her face meekly and thoughtfully bent downward; he holding her right hand in his, his left pressing on his heart, and his eyes turned to heaven." *

No one can look at this picture,

"Where his devoted heart
The wedded Luther to his Ketha gave,"

without being impressed with the moral beauty and heavenly sanctity of marriage. We experience an indefinable pleasure in

* Dr. Krauth's Conservative Reformation.

viewing Luther in this quiet, touching heart-scene, in contrast with his previous lonely and stormy life. It is like passing from the bleak, cold desolation of winter into the genial and flowery spring. And then we feel, too, the meaning and moral influences of that quiet bridal scene in the household chapel in Wittenberg. It was there Luther laid the foundation of a family in the true German and evangelical spirit. "From the Augustine cloister at Wittenberg, which had now become the residence of Luther and his family, sprang the noblest germ of social morality, and of the purest spirit of German domestic life. This cloister-home became the ideal type of numberless families of Protestant Germany, and especially of those numerous families of evangelical ministers to whom German society is so largely indebted for morality and piety." *

* Gelzer's Life of Luther.

It was as decided a step against Romanism as the burning of the Papal Bull; for it was a solemn proclamation to the world of the divine ordination of marriage for priest and people, and a practical protest by the leader of the Reformation against the enormous evils of celibacy. No wonder the Romanists raised such a hue and cry against Luther, and well-nigh overwhelmed him with all sorts of calumnies. Some said that "Antichrist would be the offspring of such a union; for it was predicted that he would be born of a monk and a nun." To this Erasmus replied, with a sarcastic smile: "If the prophecy be true, what thousands of antichrists must already exist in the world."

But while the Romanists denounced Luther for his marriage, there were many friends who commended his course, and offered him their heartfelt congratulations.

Melancthon, who was at first startled by this bold step, afterwards said, with that sweet, impressive voice to which even his enemies listened with respect, "It is false and slanderous to maintain that there is anything unbecoming in Luther's marriage. I think that in marrying he must have done violence to his own wishes, impelled thereto by conscience. A married life is one of humility, but it is also a holy state, if there be any such in the world; and the Scriptures everywhere represent it as honorable and desirable in the eyes of the Lord."

Luther was happy in this union. He used to say that the happiest life on earth is with a pious, good wife; in peace and quiet, contented with a little, and giving God thanks. Of his gentle and loving Ketha, he said: "I value her more than the kingdom of France or the wealth of the

Venetians." He could say, after years of experience, and from his very heart:

> "A wife becomes the truest, tenderest friend,
> The balm of comfort and the source of joy,
> Thro' every various turn of life the same."

The first three years of his wedded life were spent in the quiet enjoyment of his home, with his beloved Ketha by his side. Those years of retirement were not lost, as some supposed, for Luther was schooled in heart culture and social refinement, and the asperities of his nature were softened by the gentle and affectional companionship and ministries of Ketha. She won his esteem by her mental culture, and charmed his heart by her womanly graces. She consoled him in his depressions by repeating passages from the Bible, relieved him from all household cares, worked his portrait in embroidery, and, in his leisure moments, amused him by the *naïveté* of her questions. Luther's account of this is quite amusing. He says: "The first year of married life is an odd business. At meals, where you used to be alone, you are yourself and somebody else. My Ketha used to sit with me when I was at work. She thought she ought not to be silent. She did not know what to say, so she would ask me:

"'Herr doctor, is not the master of the ceremonies in Prussia the brother of the margrave?'"

She was an odd woman.

"Doctor," she said to him one day, "how is it that under popery we prayed so often and so earnestly, and now our prayers are cold and seldom?"

Ketha might have spoken for herself. Luther, to the last, spent hours every day in prayer. He advised her to read the Bible a little more. She said she had read enough of it, and knew half of it by heart.

Catharine, as is common with an affectionate wife, was too anxious about her husband, for which Luther would sometimes gently and playfully reprove her. On one occasion he shut himself up for three days in his study. Catharine, feeling very much troubled, looked for him all over the house, knocking at every door, but without success. At last she sent for a locksmith, who forced open the study-door, and there she found Luther, absorbed in his commentary on the twenty-second Psalm. She kindly reproved him for causing her so much anxiety; but he, pointing to the Bible, said: "Do you think I was doing anything bad? Do you not know that I must work as long as it is day, for the night cometh in which no man can work?"

On another occasion, in answer to an anxious letter from his wife, he wrote:

"To my gracious lady, Catharine Luther,

my dear wife, who torments herself unnecessarily, grace and peace in our Lord Jesus Christ. Dear Ketha, thou oughtest to read what St. John says in the catechism upon the confidence we ought to have in God. Thou art tormenting thyself, as if He were not all-powerful, and could not produce new Doctor Martins by the dozen, if the old one should be drowned in the Saale, or perish in any other manner. There is One who takes better care of me than thou, or even the angels of heaven can do. He sits at the right hand of his Father, and is all-powerful. Then quiet thyself. Amen."

During the earlier years of his married life Luther was very poor. According to Michelét, his income never exceeded one hundred and eight dollars. This may seem strange, considering the immense sale of his writings, and his eminent position in the eyes of all Europe. But owing to a "conscientious whim," he would not take anything for his manuscripts, and he received no fixed salary from the university. About two years after his marriage, writing to a friend who had requested a loan of him, he said: "You ask me for eight florins. Where on earth am I to get eight florins? As you know, I am compelled to live with the strictest economy, and yet my want of means, perhaps my want of care, has compelled me to contract, during the past year, debts amounting to more than a hundred florins, which I must somehow and sometime repay to various persons."

Indeed, the straitened circumstances of Luther obliged him to turn his hand to manual labor in order to obtain his bread. Speaking of this, he remarked: "Since among us barbarians there is no man of art to instruct us in better things, I and my servant Wolfgang have set ourselves to the business of *turning*, in our leisure moments."

And yet, in all the privations and anxieties of almost abject poverty, Luther was happy — happy in his faith, and happy in his family. Writing to his friend Sliepel, he said: "Catharine, my dear rib, salutes thee. She is quite well, thank God; gentle, obedient, and kind in all things, far beyond all my hopes. I would not exchange my poverty with her for all the riches of Crœsus without her."

What we think and feel of such a wedded life is best expressed in Luther's own words: "There are no ties of society more beautiful, more elevating, and happier than a well-assorted marriage. It is a pleasure to behold two people living together in wedlock in harmony and love." And such was Luther's married life.

As they came from the chapel at Wittenberg, with the benediction yet fresh upon their wedded union, Luther might have expressed his feelings in those touching words of the poet:

"My bride,
My wife, my life. Oh, we will walk this world
Yok'd in all exercise of noble aim,
And so through those dark gates across the wild
That no man knows."

And they did so walk. Their first affection acquired greater depth and intensity by the vanishing away of all that was merely ideal or fanciful. And the very trials of life deepened their mutual sympathies, and strengthened the clasping bonds of a sanctified love. It is manifest that in a union so intimate and life-long, revealing every phase of character and mood of temper, there will often be felt the need of the love that "is not easily provoked, which suffereth long, and is kind"— which has power to invest the being loved with its own beauty, transforming seeming blemishes into fancied virtues. No doubt there was something of this in Catharine's experience with a man like Luther, so full of cares and troubles from without, and withal so quick and sharp and impulsive; but she could say:

> " My love doth so approve him,
> That even his stubbornness, his checks and frowns,
> Have grace and favor in them."

Such a love, hallowed by religion, is the very life of marriage,— the very bond of perfectness. It is the fragrant blossom that will not only gladden the heart, but beautify the humblest home with the ministries of peace and charity. And so Luther and his beloved Ketha, by being *one* in Christ, maintained this affectional and life-long unity. Jesus, who came to open heavenly mansions into our earthly habitations, was their ever welcome and abiding guest, and the atmosphere of their home was redolent of His heavenly spirit. Thus they grew in personal excellence, mutual affinity, and spiritual oneness, to the end of life. This assimilative growth in true Christian marriage is beautifully expressed in those exquisite lines of Tennyson:

"Yet in the long years liker must they grow;
  The man be more of woman, she of man:
  He gain in sweetness and in moral height,
  Nor lose the wrestling thews that throw the world;
  She mental breadth, nor fail in childward care:
  Move as the double-natured poet each:
  Till at the last she set herself to man
  Like perfect music unto noble words."

LUTHER
SINGING WITH HIS FAMLY.

.

LUTHER SINGING AT HOME—INTRODUCTION OF THE GERMAN CHURCH HYMNS AND CHANTS.

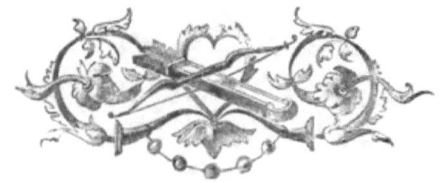

LUTHER SINGING WITH HIS FAMILY.

"God setteth the solitary in families."

THE Psalmist indicates a divine purpose in placing the individual man in domestic relations, and suggests the meaning and importance of the family. Luther was a scholar, a thinker, a Reformer, before he had a home. But how all his powers and sympathies were quickened and intensified by the new affections and solicitudes of a husband and a father! What a new life he felt in the lives of his children; nay, what depths were opened, what chords were touched, what enlarged vision was given by their departure from earth!

Luther used to say that "many children are a sign of God's blessing; and hence you may see why Duke George has never had any." Luther himself was certainly not wanting in this token of heaven's favor. He had six children: John, Elizabeth, Madeleine, Martin, Paul, and Margaret. And notwithstanding his studies, and his many labors and anxieties for the Church, he not only found time to sport with his children, but was ever inventing new plays for their diversion and amusement. And yet, child as he was with his children in their sports and pleasures, he never lost sight of the divine order and religiousness of the household. He was careful to rear his children in the nurture and admonition of the Lord, and daily repeated with them the Ten Commandments, the Creed, and the Lord's

Prayer. He was, moreover, very strict in the Christian discipline of his children; and the first law of his house was their trustful subjection to his will, and obedience in all things. When his son John was twelve years old, he was in some important instance disobedient, and committed some great wrong, on account of which Luther for three days refused to have anything to do with him, though he had meekly asked his forgiveness in writing. Some of his friends thought the discipline too severe. And when Catharine, Dr. Jonas, and Dr. Teutleben interceded for John, Luther said: "I would rather have my son dead than disobedient. St. Paul did not without reason say that a bishop must rule his own house well, and have obedient children, that other people may be edified through them, follow their example, and not be offended. We ministers are honored so much that we might set a good example. But our untrained children cause others to take offence, and bad boys commit sin in virtue of our privileges." *

Luther's home-life was a model of quiet simplicity. He was sociable, cheerful, and fond of innocent amusements. And notwithstanding his large and expensive family and his scanty income, he was the most generous and hospitable of men. He was surrounded at his table, not only by his children, but by a number of intimate friends. Melancthon, Jonas, Amsdorf, and others of his co-laborers, were his frequent and ever welcome guests, sharing alike in his toils and his pleasures. And as Luther was from habit and principle uncommonly abstemious, he would talk and joke and laugh while the company were enjoying the provisions of the table, as well as his crisp

* Fick's Life of Luther, translated by Prof. Loy.

humor and versatile conversation. At such times, as Audin says, he would talk of philosophy and demonology, biblical explanations and poetry, morality and antichrist. These conversations — *Tischreden, Table-Talk*, collected by his friends — make one of the most brilliant books in the world.*

The first years of Luther's married life, though cheerful and happy, were not without passing shadows of sorrow. But even these afflictions, though grievous at the time, afterwards yielded the peaceable fruits of righteousness, and only deepened and refined the affectional bonds and ministries of the home-life. In 1527, his little son John was attacked by the plague, which had made its appearance in Saxony, and was then raging in its most virulent form. In a letter to Spalatin, he writes: "My little favorite, John, does not salute thee, for he

* Froude's Times of Erasmus and Luther.

is still too ill to speak; but through me he solicits your prayers. For the last twelve days he has not eaten a morsel. 'T is wonderful to see how the poor child keeps up his spirits; he would manifestly be as gay and joyous as ever, were it not for the excess of his physical weakness. However, the crisis of his disease is now past."

Shortly after, Luther was himself attacked with severe illness, evidently brought on by the constant strain both of body and mind which he had been called to endure for many years. Recovering from a swoon into which he had fallen, he turned to his wife, and faintly said: "Dear Ketha, where is my little darling, my little John?" The child, when brought to him, smiled upon its father, who went on, speaking feebly, and with tears: "My poor, dear little boy, I commend thee heartily to our Lord; thee and thy good mother, my beloved Ketha.

I leave you nothing; but God, who feeds the ravens, will care for you,— He who is the father of the fatherless, and the widow's God. Preserve them, O God! teach them as Thou hast taught me!"

About six months after this sickness, Ketha gave Luther a daughter; but her stay on earth was short — like an angel's visit, or a vision of the night.

> "E'er sin could blight or sorrow fade,
> Death came with friendly care;
> The op'ning bud to heaven conveyed,
> And bade it blossom there."

Luther wrote to a friend: "My little rosebud daughter Elizabeth is dead: 't is wonderful how sick at heart her loss has made me. I feel a mere woman, so great is my sadness. I could never have dreamed that a man's soul could be touched with such tenderness, even towards his child."

These early shadows of affliction and death in Luther's family passed away, and left the home with a serener light and a warmer love; for the overshadowing cloud of death, as it passed away, was radiant with the bow that

"Spans the earth, and forms a pathway to the skies."

We pass now to a peculiar feature of the great Reformer's domestic life, as illustrated by Kœnig's picture of

LUTHER SINGING AT HOME.

It is surely not without interest to know, of a great thinker or worker, a great Teacher or Reformer, that there was in him, over and above all his special gifts and endowments of mind, a sensitiveness to the power of music. This is notable in the great Apostle of the Gentiles, who was not only a singer himself, but urged so lovingly upon his converts the singing of "psalms, and hymns, and spiritual songs;" intimating that without music their ritual would be cold and dead. Yes, in Paul, no less than in the greatest of his followers, in Augustine, in Luther, in the Wesleys, we may see a great example of the power of music, and learn to acknowledge in that power a great gift of God.

The artist conducts us into Luther's "Chantry in the House." Surrounded by his children and a few friends, he is practising the first evangelical church melodies. The man before the music-stand, with a guitar in his hand, is Walter, the Electoral Chapel-Master; on the left is the Chanter, holding an open sheet of music; on the right is Mathesius, a very intimate friend.

The picture not only gives us a glimpse of Luther's enjoyment of music in his family, but suggests how much that introduction of German church music had to do with the furtherance of evangelical religion. Luther was not only fond of music, but was really an enthusiast in this, as in everything that he loved. It made him a poet and hymnist, and his songs were the expression of the inmost heart of the German people. We find scattered through his writings many fragmentary and beautiful sentiments about music.

"Music is one of the noblest gifts of God. It is a good antidote against temptation and evil thoughts."

"Music is the best cordial to a person in sadness: it soothes, quickens, and refreshes the heart."

"I have always loved music. He that is skilled in this art is possessed of good qualities, and can be employed in any thing."

Perhaps the most significant of all his passages on music is the following:

"I am fully of the opinion, and am not ashamed to maintain, that, next to theology, music takes the highest rank in the sciences; because it alone, after theology, does that which otherwise theology alone does — it soothes the mind, and renders it joyful and courageous; which is an evidence that the evil one, the author of sad cares and unquiet emotions, flees at the voice of music almost as much as at the voice of theology. For this reason the prophets cultivated no art so much as that of music, and clothed their theology, not in geometry or arithmetic or astronomy, but in music."

Luther made music a part of his domestic enjoyments and household worship. John Walter says: "I have sung many a delightful hour with him; and have often observed how our beloved friend became more and more cheerful as we sang, and was so happy that it seemed he could never get enough of it. He has himself composed the chants to the Epistles and Gospels; has sung them to me, and asked my opinion. He kept me three weeks in Wittenberg, until the first German mass had been chanted in the parish church."

Mathesius relates that the Doctor sang at table as well as afterwards; and often, when weary and heart-sore, he would turn to his guitar or lute, and rise up refreshed and strengthened for his work. Once during Advent, in 1538, when he had the singers at table with him, and they sang some beautiful pieces, he said with deep emotion: "As our Lord pours out such noble gifts upon us in this life, how glorious will be eternal life! This is only *materia prima* — the beginning."

Luther was never happier than when, seated at his parlor-organ, the whole family united with him in singing the praises of God. It was like heaven on earth. And sometimes after such music in the family, he would say: "I love music: it elevates me and makes me better, and brings me nearer to the throne of God, where the angels cry, *Holy, holy, holy,* day and night."

There is a picture which represents Luther with his family singing their evening hymn. The eldest son, John, is playing the violin, as an accompaniment to the organ, where his father is seated, whose benignant countenance is beaming with love upon his youngest boys, who are holding fast by his instrument, and whose gladsome hearts make their eyes sparkle with joy; whilst the serene mother, with the hymn-book in her hand, bends fondly over Luther's chair; and her little daughters are standing meekly by her side, with hands clasped in silent worship. Truly, as we gaze upon that home-scene, we cannot but feel that "Religion never was designed to make our pleasures less."

"At once they sing, at once they pray,
They hear of heaven and learn the way."

LUTHER AS A HYMNIST.

But wider than his home, was the influence of his poetry and music. Luther was a poet as well as a Reformer. He performed noble deeds, which are but noble thoughts realized. In this view, Coleridge says: "He was a poet indeed, as great a poet as ever lived in any age or country; but his poetic images were so vivid that they mastered the poet's own mind. He was possessed with them, as with substances distinct from himself. Luther did not write, he acted poems." Carlyle, on "Luther's Psalms," says: "With words he had not learned to make pure music; it was by deeds of love and heroic valor that he spoke freely.... Nevertheless, in imperfect articulation, the same voice, if we listen well, is to be heard in his poems."

Luther was no doubt born a poet; but it was in times of peril and tribulation that the poetry in him blossomed into hymns. Some men

"Are cradled into poetry by wrong,
And learn in suffering, what they teach in song."

So it was with Luther. We find the translator and expounder and preacher of the word of God giving the tone as the spiritual poet of the Reformation. By the adaptation of old German poems to the service of the temple, and the translation of Latin lyrics, as well as by his own original hymns, he became the Father of psalmody—that beautiful blossom of German Protestantism.

A small collection of his hymns was first published at Wittenberg, in 1524; and another the year following. It was the one great doctrine of salvation by faith in Jesus, which he preached from the towers of Erfurt, and before the Diet of Worms, preached always and everywhere, woven into hymns and spiritual songs, that helped so wondrously the onward march of the Reformation.

Others caught the spirit of Luther, and became poets and singers. Not only in palaces, cathedrals, and cloisters, but among the common people everywhere were found the friends of the Reformation. Among this worthy class there was a notable shoemaker—one Hans Sachs, of Nuremberg. This man managed to make shoes and verses at the same time. Nuremberg, his native place, was one of the first cities of Germany to welcome the new doctrine; and soon Hans Sachs tuned his lyre to the service of the Reformed doctrine; and since the minstrel's song had ceased in the feudal castle, no music so stirred and aroused the German people as his rude Christian lyrics. According to Wetzel, about five thousand of his brave and earnest songs went out from his humble workshop, while Luther was at work upon the outposts of papal superstition. And it would be difficult to decide whether this poet of the people or the Elector of Saxony, achieved the most in the great Reformation of the sixteenth century; or to say how much Hans Sachs, by his earnest and spiritual hymns, helped Luther in his sermons and Melancthon in his epistles.

But we have now to speak mainly of Luther's hymns, and what they did for himself and the Reformation. Luther's first hymn, it is said, was occasioned by the martyrdom of two young Christian monks, who were burnt alive, at Brussels, by the Sophists :

"Flung to the heedless winds, or on the waters cast,
 Their ashes shall be watched, and gathered at the last.
 And from that scattered dust, around us and abroad,
 Shall spring a plenteous seed of witnesses for God.
 Jesus hath now received their latest living breath,
 Yet vain is Satan's boast of victory in their death.
 Still, still, though dead, they speak, and trumpet-tongued proclaim,
 To many a wakening land, the one availing Name."

This, among the hymns of Luther, is remarkable for its harmonious measure and poetical rhythm, and, like all his Christian lyrics, is full of his fire and enthusiasm and joyful trust in God.

His "Song of Praise for Redemption"

is remarkable as a condensed versification of his "Commentary on the Galatians," or as containing the essence of his own life-experience. We give the first verse:

> "Dear Christian people all rejoice,
> Each soul with joy upspringing;
> Pour forth our song with heart and voice,
> With love and gladness singing.
> Give thanks to God, our Lord above,
> Thanks for His miracle of love!
> Dearly He hath redeemed us!"

Luther's carol for Christmas, written for his own child Hans, is still sung from the dome of the Kreuz-Kirche, in Dresden, before daybreak on the morning of Christmas-day. "It refers to the custom, then and long afterwards prevalent in Germany, of making, at Christmas-time, representations of the manger with the infant Jesus."*

But the most famous of all his hymns is

---
* Evenings with the Sacred Poets, p. 98.

his noble version of Psalm XLVI., "*Ein Feste burg ist unser Gott*," which may be called the national hymn of Protestant Germany. One cannot speak of German Psalmody, or rightly appreciate Luther, without this grand poem, in which his heroic spirit unconsciously shines forth in ideal and inimitable grandeur. "*Ein Feste burg*," it is said, was composed by Luther on his way to Worms, and is a regular battle-song. Heine says: "The old cathedral trembled when it heard these novel sounds; the very rooks flew from their nests on its towers. That hymn, the Marseillaise of the Reformation, has preserved to the present day its potent spell over German hearts, and we may yet hear it thundered forth." *

Of the many translations of this memorable hymn, we select the following from

---

* Heine, in the *Revue de Deux Mondes*, 1834.

the CHURCH BOOK, as sufficiently literal, whilst it retains much of the grand rhythm of the original, and is, moreover, adapted to the music composed by Luther. The music is as soul-stirring as the hymn; and the two are so united by a common birth, sympathy and historical association, that they ought never to be separated.

LUTHER'S GREAT HYMN.

"A mighty Fortress is our God,
 A trusty shield and weapon;
He helps us free from every need
 That hath us now o'ertaken.
  The old bitter foe
  Means us deadly woe;
 Deep guile and great might
 Are his dread arms in fight,
On earth is not his equal.

"With might of ours can naught be done,
 Soon were our loss effected;
But for us fights the Valiant One
 Whom God himself elected.

> Ask ye, who is this?
> Jesus Christ it is,
> Of Sabaoth Lord,
> And there's none other God,
> He holds the field forever.
>
> "Though devils all the world should fill,
> All watching to devour us,
> We tremble not, we fear no ill,
> They cannot overpower us.
> This world's prince may still
> Scowl fierce as he will,
> He can harm us none.
> He's judged, the deed is done,
> One little word o'erthrows him.
>
> "The Word they still shall let remain,
> And not a thank have for it;
> He's by our side upon the plain,
> With his good gifts and spirit.
> Take they then our life,
> Goods, fame, child and wife;
> When their worst is done,
> They yet have nothing won:
> The Kingdom ours remaineth."

Of this hymn, Carlyle says in his own peculiar way: "It jars upon our ears; yet is there something in it like the sound of

Alpine avalanches, or the first murmur of earthquakes; in the very vastness of which dissonance a higher unison is revealed to us. Luther wrote this song in a time of blackest threatenings, — which, however, could in nowise become a time of despair. ... It is evident enough that to this man all Popes' conclaves and imperial Diets, and hosts and nations were but weak; weak as the forest, with all its strong *trees*, may be to the smallest spark of electric *fire*."

It has been justly called the battle-hymn of the Church, and the pæan of the Reformation, for it was a song of inspiration and power to Luther and others in the darkest days of the Church. On the 16th of April, as Luther approached Worms, and the old bell-towers rose to view, he stood up in his chariot, and began to sing this soul-stirring hymn. One day, when Melancthon was at Weimar, he heard a little child sing this hymn in the street, and confessed how it had comforted him. It was sung by Gustavus Adolphus for the last time on the battle-field of Lutzen, where the pious king of Sweden fell, nobly fighting for God and his country. It was sung by the camp-fires and before many a battle in the recent Prussian war, and with all the fire and enthusiasm of the times of Luther. Some one asked the Elector Frederick why he did not build fortifications in his country. He answered: "Ein Feste Burg ist unser Gott." It was this hymn that was sung in sorrow and tears over Luther's grave, and its first line was inscribed upon his tomb.

Coleridge says "that Luther did as much for the Reformation by his hymns as by his translation of the Bible." This perhaps is a little too strong; but it must be evident that the influence of his hymns was mighty and extensive in moulding popular sentiment, and uniting men in the common faith of Protestantism, who knew little of Creeds and Articles. They were to Luther himself a means of inspiration and strength in the stormy conflict through which he was called to pass, and a cheering, heavenly enjoyment in his family. We have alluded to the singing of *Ein Feste Burg* as he entered Worms. We give one other instance of his singing in time of trouble. During the Diet of Augsburg, in 1530, Luther's mental anxiety so overcame his bodily strength, that he fainted; on recovering, he said, "Come, let us defy the devil, and praise God, by singing the hymn, *Out of the depths, I cry to Thee.*" This hymn has been sung by thousands of believers in times of sickness and sorrow. It was sung in the cathedral of Wittenberg at Luther's funeral. In the very church, upon whose doors he had nailed his Theses, his sorrowing friends sang this hymn that had so stirred all Germany. It is said to have been the last Protestant hymn sung in the Strasbourg Cathedral.

It is not possible to estimate how much the hymns of Luther advanced the cause of the Reformation. The common people of Germany caught up these songs, so full of strong scriptural words, and sang them with all their hearts: so that it has been truly said that the hymns of Germany became her national liturgy. And then, unlike the idle listening to a dry and heartless litany, the people were able to understand the deep spiritual meaning of these hymns, so respondent to their soul experiences and holiest aspirations. No wonder it is said in the history of those times, that the children learned Luther's hymns in the cottage, and martyrs sang them on the scaffold. And no wonder that the Romanists hated these hymns almost as much as an open Bible, for they helped on the spread of the evangelical Church. Hence, a Roman Catholic writer says: "The hymns of Luther have ruined more souls than all his writings and sermons."

It is curious and suggestive to note how the Reformation went on its way, not only singing, but *by* singing. It is said that the Reformation was introduced into the city of Hanover, not by preachers or by books, but by the hymns of Luther which were sung among the people. It is reported that hundreds, who otherwise would never have heard the name of Luther, were brought to the true faith by means of that single hymn, "*Nun freut euch, liebe Christengemein.*"

Selnecker relates that several of these hymns having been introduced into the chapel-service of the Duke Henry of Wolfenbüttle, a priest made complaint. The duke asked what hymns he objected to. "May it please your highness, they are such as, 'Oh, that the Lord would gracious be!'" "Hold!" replied the duke; "must the devil, then, be gracious? Whose grace are we to seek, if not that of God only?" It is hardly necessary to add that the hymns continued to be sung in the chapel.

In 1529, a Romish priest preached at Lubeck, and just as he ended his homily, two boys struck up the hymn of Luther, "O God, from heaven now behold!" when the whole assembly joined as with one voice; and this was repeated whenever any one spake against the evangelical Church.*

Something like this occurred at Heidelberg. "On one occasion, a priest was about to begin the service, standing at the high altar, when a single voice led off the

* Evenings with the Poets, page 101.

beginning of the famous hymn of Paul Speratus, '*Es ist das Heil uns kommen her.*' The vast congregation immediately joined; and the elector, taking this as a sufficient suffrage of his people, proceeded to introduce the communion in both kinds; for, hitherto, Frederick, from fear of the emperor, had delayed suppressing the mass. It was Luther's hymns and tunes combined that did the work." *

A very curious incident is related of that remarkable hymn, which seemed to embody in verse the religious experience of Luther, "Song of praise for redeeming love," and which begins,

> "Dear Christian people, all rejoice,
> Each soul with joy upspringing;
> Pour forth your song with heart and voice,
> With love and gladness singing."

It is said that in 1557, a convention of

* Evenings with the Poets, page 102.

princes of the reformed religion, at Frankfort, wished to introduce a Protestant service in the Church of St. Bartholomew. A large assembly was present; but the pulpit was occupied by a priest, who proceeded to set forth the peculiar doctrines of the Romish Church. For a time the people listened in sullen silence; but at last the whole congregation rose and began to sing this hymn, till they fairly sang the priest out of the church.

In these fragmentary allusions to the hymns of Luther, as sung by people of every class, not only in schools and churches, but in the markets and fields, the streets and homes of Germany, we cannot fail to see how mighty must have been their influence upon the masses in advancing the cause of the Reformation. And then it was not only what Luther himself did in psalmody, but what he inspired others to do, who caught his spirit, embraced his doctrines, and tuned their lyres in the service of Protestantism. Wetzel, in 1718, estimated the printed German hymns at fifty-five thousand, of which sacred lyrics, Hans Sachs alone wrote about five thousand. It may not, therefore, be too much for Coleridge to say that Luther did as much for the Reformation by his hymns as by his translation of the Bible. For after all, these hymns contained the substance of God's truth, in Luther's strong, scriptural, Saxon words, and dropped in music into the hearts of the people, as dew melts into the heart of a flower.

We cannot better close this chapter of Luther's home-life than by commending to all Christians his practice of singing hymns. "Let the word of Christ dwell in you richly, in all wisdom; teaching and admonishing one another in psalms and hymns and spiritual songs, singing with grace in your hearts to the Lord."

Let every Christian sing. It will keep warm in his heart the love of Jesus, and diffuse a heavenly peace through the soul. And especially should Christians sing in times of depression and sorrow. So did Jesus. In that memorable night in which Christ and his disciples went out to the garden, they sang a hymn. Before Jesus were the agony and the cross and Calvary; before the apostles was the sad thought of separation: and yet they sang, not some mournful song, but a hymn of praise and exultation, such as, "The Lord is my strength and my song, and is become my salvation."

So Luther, whenever the sky was dark and threatening, would say, Come, let us sing the forty-sixth Psalm. As he approached Worms, as already mentioned, he rose in his chariot, and sang *Ein Feste Burg ist unser Gott.* During the Diet of Augsburg, when fainting with mental anxiety, he said, "Let us praise God by singing the hymn, 'Out of the depths I cry to Thee.'" And so should any Christian, when sad and despondent, sing hymns of praise. It will calm the troubled soul and soothe the aching heart. He will go forth with a firmer step and a more hopeful spirit to his Gethsemane and Calvary, if he goes singing, "Why art thou cast down, oh my soul? and why art thou disquieted within me? hope thou in God; for I shall yet praise Him, who is the health of my countenance and my God."

Let Christians, like Luther, sing in the family. It will quicken the social virtues, deepen the home affections, and beautify the household with peace and harmony. One of the sweetest memories of a Christian home is the recollection of the hymns and music of family worship.

In Kœnig's picture, we see Luther exercising himself and family in the first evangelical church melodies. He was specially concerned for the training of children in singing church music. In the preface to his first collection of hymns, he says: "These hymns are set to music in four parts, for no other reason than that the young people, who ought at all events to be instructed in music and other proper arts, might be rid of their silly songs, and, instead, have something good and useful as becometh the young. I should be glad to see all arts, and especially music, employed in the service of God." Not only did Luther teach his own children music, but insisted upon its being taught in the schools of the Church. "A school-master must be able to sing, otherwise I will have nothing to do with him."

It would be well for Christians of our day to follow the example of Luther in this peculiarity of his home-life. Let there be music in the family. The singing of hymns is one of the most eminent ways in which the household can have a conscious presence of Jesus, and realize the sweet unity of peace and love. Let the children learn to sing. The spring-time of life, like that of nature, may fitly begin with song. The hymns of the Church sung by the child are woven into the creed of the man. The great doctrines of Christianity liquefied by song, may flow into the young heart by hymns, and abide there as "a well of water, springing up into everlasting life." Many a child has found Jesus in the words and music of a Christian hymn. The sweet invitation of the Saviour, *Suffer little children to come unto me*, has been sung into the young heart, and touched it with a responsive love and consecration. How beautiful the story of the little girl thus brought to Jesus, who, as she lay in her last sickness, looked up to her mother with a hopeful smile, and grasping her hand, said: "Mother, sing to me of heaven!" These words of the dying child have been thus versified for the young by an American poet:

"Oh, sing to me of heaven, when I am called to die !
Sing songs of holy ecstasy to waft my soul on high.
Then to my raptured ears let one sweet song be given ;
Let music charm me last on earth, and greet me first in heaven ! "

SUMMER JOYS WITH HIS FAMILY.

LUTHER'S JOYS OF SUMMER IN THE BOSOM OF HIS FAMILY.

SUMMER JOYS WITH HIS FAMILY.

IN Kœnig's pictured life of Luther, there is a domestic garden-scene, in which the great Reformer appears with his family, encompassed with the fruits and flowers of summer. The artist's work would have been incomplete without this beautiful memorial of Luther; for his heart ever opened in the free air, in the sights and shows of the passing seasons; and to his poetical fancy nature was full of symbols and spiritual suggestions.

"The picture shows him in the enjoyment of all that imparts delight to summer, with his household and his most familiar friends about him. It is a charming scene of innocent festivity which the artist here brings before the eye. Under a trellis, mantled with vines loaded with rich clusters of grapes, the party is assembled at sunset. Luther holds out his hands to his youngest child, who, by the aid of his mother, is tottering towards his father, with a bunch of grapes weighing down his little hands. The oldest boy, mounted on a light ladder, hands down the grapes, which Madeleine receives in her apron. The third boy is bringing to his father a cluster remarkable for its size; the second son is playing with the dog — perhaps that very dog which Luther said had 'looked upon many books.' The ground is covered with melons. One of Luther's friends plays upon the flute, another sketches a basket of beautiful fruit; two of them sit beneath the arbor, and two others wander about the garden in friendly converse. Through an arch in the wall, the river is seen winding gently along, under the last rays of the declining sun. What a change from the time of scourging before the crucifix!"*

This is a fine description of the beautiful picture; but the young reader may want to know something more about the dog, which seems to look so intently, and with such a sober face, at that large bunch of grapes which the third boy is showing to his father. There is a sad and oldish look about his face; and we are disposed to believe that he is the same dog which Luther brought with him from Wartburg, as a gift from the keeper of the castle, and that died of old age, after fifteen years spent at his master's feet, where he was wont to re-

---

* Dr. Krauth's Conservative Reformation, page 34.

pose while Luther was writing. Hence, Luther said, in allusion to the theologians who boasted of having seen so many books: "Aye, and my dog also has seen many books,— more, probably, than Faber himself, who has nothing in his mouth but Fathers and councils. I know that Faber has seen many books: I do not envy him his glory."

It was a happy idea of the artist to picture this domestic garden-scene of Luther's summer joys with his family, for it gives us at once a glimpse of the great Reformer in his love of home, of children, of nature and flowers. He was both a poet and a philosopher. Some one says of Hume, that he could fetch you the leg of a metaphysical notion from the Central Africa of Duns Scotus or Thomas Aquinas in the twinkling of an eye; but he seems never to have gone out of his closet long enough to see

what there was in nature, or whether there was any such thing as *nature* at all."*
Not so with Luther. He was as great a lover of nature as he was of music and poetry. He looked upon all natural objects with a poetic eye, and to his imagination the outer world was full of beautiful symbols and spiritual suggestions.

> "And so the very flowers seemed silent hymns,
> And by their aspect of persuasive bloom
> Remind him oft of Eden, long no more;
> Or bid him muse on what the world may be
> When second paradise again shall dawn." †

Doubtless botany has its value; but the flowers knew how to preach divinity before men knew how to dissect and botanize them; for long before botany as a science was dreamed of, Luther had divined the principle of vegetable life. He said: "The principle of marriage runs through all cre-

---
* Hudson's Lectures on Shakspeare.
† Luther: A Poem. By Robert Montgomery.

ation, and flowers as well as animals are male and female." But he loved nature more as a poet than as a scientist, as is manifest from his many poetical sentiments about nature, and his rare enjoyment of the garden and all natural objects; for poetry is but the true and the good seen under the aspect of the beautiful. And so to Luther often the commonest thing becomes an Aaron's rod, and buds and blossoms out into poetry; and in this respect he was like Burns, to whom the sight of a mountain daisy unsealed the fountains of his nature, and who embalmed the "bonny gem" in the beauty of his spirit.

The summer-garden sometimes drew from him a strain of sentiment and feeling as beautiful as a finished piece of poetry. One day, in early spring, as he was watching the swelling buds, he exclaimed:

"Praise be to God the Creator, who out

of a dead world makes all alive again. See those shoots, how they sprout and swell! Image of the resurrection of the dead! Winter is death; summer is the resurrection. Between them lie spring and autumn, as the period of uncertainty and change. The proverb says:

> 'Trust not a day
> Ere birth of May.'

Let us pray our Father in heaven to give us this day our daily bread."

At another time he said: " We are in the dawn of a new era; we are beginning to think something of the natural world which was ruined in Adam's fall. We are learning to see all around us the greatness and glory of the Creator. We can see the Almighty hand, the infinite goodness, in the humblest flower. We praise Him, we glorify Him; we recognize in creation the power of his word. He spoke, and it was there. The stone of the peach is hard; but the soft kernel swells, and bursts it when the time comes. An egg — what a thing is that! If an egg had never been seen in Europe, and a traveller had brought one from Calcutta, how would the world have wondered!"

And again: "If a man could make a single rose, we should give him an empire; yet roses, and flowers no less beautiful, are scattered in profusion over the world, and no one regards them." *

In writing to his friend Link, at Nuremberg, he asks him to send him seeds for the garden, and says: "If Satan and his imps rave and roar, I shall laugh at him, and admire and enjoy, to the Creator's praise, God's blessings in the garden." On another occasion, he wrote to Spalatin: "I

* Froude's Times of Erasmus and Luther.

have planted my garden, and made a fountain in the centre of it. Come and see us, and you shall be crowned with lilies and roses." When the seeds sent him by his old friend Link began to sprout, he wrote to him, with the simple joy of a child: "My melons are growing; my gourds are filling up. What a blessing!"

Luther had a pure, sanctified poetical feeling, sensitive to every phase of natural beauty; and to this inner, spiritual vision the world was full of symbols and suggestions of divine things. Once, he looks out from his solitary Patmos, the castle of Coburg, in the middle of the night; the great vault of immensity, long flights of clouds sailing through it,—dumb, gaunt, huge; who supports all that? None ever saw the pillars of it; yet it is supported. God supports it. We must know that God is great, that God is good, and trust where we cannot see. Returning home from Leipsic once, he is struck by the beauty of the harvest-fields. How it stands, that golden, yellow corn, on its fair taper stem, its golden head bent, all rich and waving there! the meek earth, at God's bidding, has produced it once again — the bread of man.*

It is said of Linnæus, that he sometimes studied the flowers on his knees. So did Luther. We are told that he often knelt down to admire them more closely. "Poor violet," he would say; "what a perfume you exhale! It would, however, be still more agreeable if Adam had not sinned. Oh, rose, how I admire your colors, which would be still more brilliant had it not been for the sin of the first man! How thy beauty, O lily, effaces that of the princes of the world! What, then, would it be, if Adam

---

* Spiritual Portrait of Luther, by Thomas Carlyle, page 216.

had not disobeyed his Creator?" He believed that after Adam's fall God deprived the earth of a portion of the gifts he had first imparted to it. "Nature, however," said he, "has not been niggardly towards man. The murmuring of rivulets, the odor of flowers, the breath of winds, and the rustling of leaves, are made so many hymns chanted to the Creator's praise; whereas man forgets Him altogether since his sin! Oh! man, how great would have been your happiness had not Adam sinned! You would have seen and admired God in all His works; and the smallest flower or plant would have been for you the exhaustless source of meditation on the goodness and magnificence of Him who created the world. If God has made the rocks bud forth such flowers, with such sweet perfume, and such brilliant colors that no painter can successfully imitate them, what endless variety of flowers, of all colors,—blue, yellow, red,—could not He produce from the earth?"*

Luther had little sympathy or patience with men who were insensible to the beauties of nature. He once said: "Poor Erasmus, what do you care how the fruit is formed, matured, or developed. You know nothing of the beauty or grandeur of creation. . . . Tell Erasmus to admire these wonders; but they are above his capacity. He looks on creatures as a calf looks at a new door." †

DOMESTIC GARDEN-SCENE.

In Kœnig's picture, we see Luther and his family and a few friends in the social enjoyments of summer. He is himself a child among the flowers and the children. He forgets all his troubles in the innocent

---

* Life of Martin Luther, by Audin, 368.
† *Siehet er die Creaturen an, wie die Kühe ein Neuthor.*

pleasures of the garden, into which he enters with such uncommon zest and merriment. It is said of Dr. Chalmers, that in the darkest hours of the Free Church of Scotland, he would say to his children, "Come, let us go out and play ball or fly the kite;" and often in the sport the children could not keep up with the father. So, in times of the greatest anxiety and suspense, when the whole future of the Reformation work seemed trembling in the balance, Luther would turn to his children. As an instance of this, and as opening a window into the great man's heart in this gardenscene, we give here, as the most fitting place, his letter to his little son John. It reveals his love and sympathy for his children, even in the most troublous times. It is one of the most beautiful pages in the life of Luther. He was confined in the castle of Coburg while the Imperial Diet at Augsburg was in session, before which the Reformed Confession was about to be presented. Walking one day in Coburg, he stopped before a toy-shop, and was overcome with tender thoughts of home and his little son. On returning to the castle, he laid aside the second Psalm, which he was translating into German, and took up his pen and wrote this beautiful letter to his son John, then four years old:

"Grace and peace in Christ, my dear little son. I am very glad to know that you learn your lessons well and love to say your prayers. Keep on doing so, my little boy, and when I come home, I will bring you something pretty from the fair. I know of a beautiful garden, where there are a great many children in fine little coats, and they go under the trees and gather beautiful apples and pears, cherries and plums; they sing, and run about, and are as happy as they can be. Sometimes they ride about on nice little ponies, with golden bridles and silver saddles. I asked the man whose garden it is, What little children are these? And he told me, They are little children who love to pray and learn, and are good. Then I said: My dear sir, I have a little boy at home; his name is little Hans Luther; would you let him come into the garden, too, to eat some of these nice apples and pears, and ride on these fine little ponies, and play with these children? The man said: If he loves to say his prayers, and learn his lesson, and is a good boy, he may come. And Philip and Jocelin may come too; and when they are all together, they can play on the fife and drum and lute and all kinds of instruments, and skip about, and shoot with little cross-bows. He then showed me a beautiful mossy place in the middle of the garden, for them to skip about in, with a great many golden fifes and drums, and silver cross-bows. The children had not yet had their dinner, and I could not wait to see them play, but I said to the man: My dear sir, I will go away and write all about it to my little son, John, and tell him to be fond of saying his prayers, and learn much, and be good, so that he may come into this garden; but he has a Cousin Lehne, whom he must bring along with him. The man said, Very well; go write to him. Now, my dear little son, love your lessons and your prayers, and tell Philip and Jocelin to do so too, that you may all come to the garden. May God bless you. Give Cousin Lehne my love, and kiss her for me."

This simple and touching letter opens another window in the heart of Luther, and illumines this loving family gathering in the garden. The picture shows us only one of the many garden-scenes in his life. The neat little parlor, with its windows shaded by vines instead of silken drapery, opened into a garden where Catharine and Luther often walked in pleasant converse. At one time you might see him working in his garden, going to the fountain to get water for his flower-plots, and as proud of his blooming shrubbery almost as of his translation of the New Testament. Pfizer says: "He loved his garden so much because, when assailed by the devil, he could take up the spade, and thus laughing in his sleeve at Satan, escape from him among flowers."* At another time, Catharine would pluck a branch loaded with cherries, and put it upon his table in primitive simplicity; or she would treat him with a mess of fish from his own little pond in the garden; and such little attentions of deli-

* Gustav. Pfizer.

cate kindness, not only gave her so much innocent pleasure, but awakened in him feelings of grateful love, and sent his thoughts singing to the Father of mercies and fountain of all good.

One beautiful spring day, Luther and Catharine were walking in the garden for some time, in silent admiration of the blossoming trees and new-born flowers, and in quiet enjoyment of the sweetness and beauty of the scene, when Luther suddenly exclaimed: "Glory to God, who calls all nature to new life! See those trees! they are already filled with fruit. What a striking image of the resurrection. Look at this flower; it was broken at the stem last August. When all other flowers are withered, this is fresh and fair, and therefore it is called *amaranthus*, and in winter people make garlands of it. So is God's word; it will never lose its freshness, never wither nor decay."

One evening, about sunset, he saw a little bird perched upon a tree, and settling itself for the night. "That little bird," said he, "has chosen its place of rest; above it are the stars and deep heaven of worlds, yet it has folded its little wings; gone trustfully to rest there as in its home, and leaves God to think of its to-morrow."

A little bird once built itself a nest in his garden. Sometimes the passers-by would frighten it away. Seeing this, the Doctor would say: "Ah, dear little bird, do not flee; from my heart I wish thee no harm, if thou couldst but believe me. So we often do not trust in God, who, so far from doing us any evil, has given us everything, even his own Son."

Luther had a peculiarly scriptural and illustrative way of speaking to his family, turning the every-day things of life to religious uses and ends. One evening, as the cows were returning from pasture, he said: "Behold! there go our preachers; there are our milk-bearers, butter-bearers, cheese- and wool-bearers, which do daily preach to us faith towards God, that we should trust in Him as our loving Father, who careth for us, and will maintain and nourish us." Playing with one of his children, who was full of the gayety and sports of childhood, he said: "Thou art the innocent little simpleton of our Lord, under grace, and not under the law. Thou hast no fear and no anxiety; all that thou doest is well done. We old simpletons torment ourselves by endless disputes upon the Word. We ought to follow the example of little children, and simply trust the word of the Lord." One day, looking at little Martin playing with his dog, he said: "This boy preacheth God's words by his deeds and acts; for God saith: 'Have dominion over the fishes of the sea and over the beasts of the field.' See how the dog putteth up with everything from him."

Luther with his children in the garden turned its very beauty into a ministry of spiritual culture and refinement, getting lessons of trust and simplicity for the children from the birds and the flowers; making the garden, so fresh and musical about them, suggestive of something yet more beautiful to come. And so, even to the children, with the blue sky bending over them as if in silent benediction, the summer-garden became the symbol of a sunnier and happier paradise.

One day his children were admiring the color of a peach, then a rare fruit, of which Luther had received a present. "Look you, my children," said the Doctor; "this is but a feeble image of what you may one day see on high. Before their fall, Adam and Eve had peaches as beautiful as this, and even more so, compared with which our peaches are but wild pears." In this delicate and somewhat sentimental way he turned the thoughts of the children, in sympathy with his own, to the bright future of this world. He gave them to understand that what they so much admired in the beauty of the flowers and the song of the birds and the glory of the summer sky, was but a faint aurora of the new heavens and the new earth, wherein dwelleth righteousness.

In this way Luther set his home-life on earth in spiritual and hopeful sympathy with the home in heaven. The old Romans held the face of the new-born child to the stars, indicating by the touching superstition that it was destined to a higher life beyond the skies. Luther, in his family religion, gave the true expression to that dim pagan yearning, in the baptismal welcome and Christian consecration of the child; embosoming the young immortal in the love of God, surrounding it with all that is pure and beautiful in nature and art, and stimulating its spiritual development by the genial and sunny atmosphere of a cheerful household piety, so that the child, under such warm and heavenly ministries, might grow in the nurture of the Lord, and open its heart to heaven as naturally as the flower opens its beauty to the sun. And such a genial, happy Christian home becomes a living and sanctifying memory, so that the child in all the after-life will look back to it with the sentiment —

"The thought of those first years in me doth breed
Perpetual benediction."

Luther, in his summer joys with his family in the garden, gave to Germany and to all lands the true ideal type of a cheerful, happy, Christian home. And if we take with us through life the memory and influence of our early years, how important that the home of childhood should be one of beauty and culture and refinement, of innocent pleasure and cheerful hope, sanctified by the word of God and prayer; so that the youth and the man, even to old age, may live in the past, the soul's first ideal, and bless Heaven

> ". . . . for those first affections,
> Those shadowy recollections
> Which, be they what they may,
> Are yet the fountain light of all our day."

WINTER PLEASURES.

LUTHER'S WINTER PLEASURES.

WINTER PLEASURES.

WE pass from that summer garden-scene to the winter fireside. And to a man like Luther, full of sympathy with nature in her ever-varying moods and seasons, winter would bring its own pleasures as well as summer. Winter is specially the season for home-joys, as it is for mental development and progress. Our own Prescott has said, in his peculiar way, "I think better of snow-storms since I find that, though they keep a man's body indoors, they bring his mind out." And while it is true that the soil is more fruitful as you approach the tropics, what is taken out of the land is put into the man as you touch the snow. And winter, outwardly so cold and ungenial, has its own peculiar blessings, especially for the family. It develops and strengthens the social affections. The frowning face of nature, like the dark cloud of adversity, lends a charm to all the inner life, and augments the sympathies and pleasures of home.

From what we have seen of Luther in the garden, we can easily fancy how he would gather the family more closely and lovingly about the fireside, and sit in the warm light of a winter evening; and how, as he listens to the cold bleak winds, he would feel his heart warmed with grateful praise for his mercies, and touched with pity for the poor and needy. Perhaps, as the snow falls and beats about the home, and his heart grows tender in its thankfulness, and reaches out into the dreary storm, he would think of the little bird which he saw going to sleep on a tree in his summer-garden, and wonder what has become of it; and, if not in the words, yet with the feelings of Burns, he might say:

> "Ilk happing bird, wee, helpless thing,
> That in the merry month o' spring
> Delighted us to hear thee sing,—
> What comes o' thee?
> Whaur wilt thou cower thy chittering wing,
> And close thy ee?"

At all events, we think it likely Luther would moralize about the things of winter as he did in the summer-garden. The snow-flakes would send his thoughts heavenward, whence the wonder came; and it would be natural for one so poetical to see in them a beautiful testimony to the Sermon on the Mount, and, by a natural suggestion, to extend Christ's great lesson of summer into winter. He might not consider the snow-flakes as so many regular crystals, shaped with the most delicate art into hexagons,—clustered foliage of interlacing network,—but looking at the snow, as it robes the fields, to keep warm the seeds and germs of the coming spring, and how softly this winter robe, woven like gossamer by the divine fingers, falls like a dream over the frosty earth, gently as the evening dew upon summer flowers, he would see in this the same Providence that gives to the lily its summer beauty, and cares for the birds of the air. And so the winter would touch his heart with filial trust in his heavenly Father, whose hand reaches down to the snow-flakes as to the brilliant constellations of heaven; and for him, in dreary winter, as in blooming summer, there is no anxious thought for the morrow. For not a snow-flake or a sparrow can fall without his heavenly Father, and the very hairs of his head are all numbered.

HOME IN WINTER.

The transition from the summer garden to the winter fireside is natural and easy. And we feel something of the exhilaration of the season as we see Luther with his family on Christmas eve. Gelzer, following Kœnig's pictorial life of Luther, says: "Upon the pleasures of summer follow those of winter,— the Christmas festival,— and the garden which now delights Luther's eyes are his children, whom he looked upon as God's greatest blessing." One day, when his friend Justus Jonas hung over the table a branch loaded with beautiful cherries, in remembrance of the creation, and praised the Lord for such delicious fruits of the earth, Luther said: "Why do you not much rather consider this in your children — fruits which are more excellent, beautiful and noble creatures of God than any fruits of trees?" He spoke of children as the choicest gifts of heaven. When John, his first child was born, with a heart overflowing with gratitude, he wrote at once to his old friend Spalatin, informing him of the joyous event: "God be praised, I am a father. Catharine, my dear wife, has presented me with a son. I am, thank God, a father. I wish with all my heart that heaven may give you the same and even greater happiness, for you are much better than I."

Luther was never happier than when surrounded by his wife and children. He seemed to be in the most delightful sympathy with all their curious fancies and simple merriment. He would often gather them about him, and with a few congenial friends spend the evening in singing and music. He once said to Melancthon: "We ought not always to serve God with labor, but also with resting and recreation." It was in the sunshine of his children, in their sports and laughter and singing, that the great Reformer forgot the storm of the outer world; and the cloud of anxious cares about the Church melted away in the sunny memories of his own innocent and happy childhood. Many a time during those dark days of the Reformation, Luther might have found in those beautiful words of Longfellow the truest expression of his thoughts and feelings:

> "Come to me, O ye children!
>   For I hear you at your play;
> And the questions that perplexed me
>   Have vanished quite away.
>
> "Ye open the eastern windows,
>   That look towards the sun,—
> Where thoughts are singing swallows,
>   And the brooks of morning run.
>
> "In your hearts are the birds and the sunshine,
>   In your thoughts the brooklet's flow,
> But in mine is the wind of Autumn
>   And the first fall of the snow.

"Come to me, O ye children!
   And whisper in my ear
What the birds and the winds are singing
   In your sunny atmosphere.

"For what are all our contrivings,
   And the wisdom of our books,
When compared with your caresses,
   And the gladness of your looks?"

CHRISTMAS EVE.

Luther restored to Protestant Christendom the true ideal and experience of the old Christmas festival. All life to him was now a festival of joy and praise for the holy child Jesus. "He had found the Christ; and when he was not kneeling with the shepherds, he was singing with the angels." And this new consciousness and experience of a personal, present Saviour, illumined and sanctified the memory of his early Christmas days. In his old age, he speaks of his school-years at Magdeburg with delightful reminiscences of Christmas: "At the season when the Church keeps the festival of Christ's birth, we scholars went through the hamlets, from house to house, singing in quartette the familiar hymns about Jesus, the little child born at Bethlehem."

And not only to Luther, but to all the Protestant families of Germany, Christmas eve came with a new welcome of joy. "The eyes of men grew bright, and those of women were suffused with tears of gratitude, and children shouted for gladness at the mention of the name of one who had led back the race to the cradle, and taught them how to bow there, as did the shepherds, in childlike trust — trust not in the mother, but in her holy child." *

In one of Kœnig's happiest illustrations, we have Luther with his family on Christ-

* Conservative Reformation.

mas eve. The Christmas-tree, in olden times, represented the birth of the *Christ-Kindlein*. At the foot of the tree was the manger, with the mother and her holy child. But these have disappeared, and the only figure remaining is the announcing angel, at the top of the tree, which is sometimes mistaken for the Christ-child, and which is usually taken down, as soon as the child-drama of Christmas begins, and given to the angel of the household — the best of the children.

The artist has given us a true picture of Luther with his family on Christmas eve. In the centre stands the Christmas-tree all ablaze with lights, and hung with cakes and fruits and toys, that so delight the tastes and fancies of children. Near by Luther stands Catharine, leaning on his shoulder, with her hand clasped in his, and looking into his face with all the devotion and tenderness of a wife and mother. On the left is Melancthon, directing Martin, the oldest boy, how to hit an apple on the tree with his cross-bow. On the right is Aunt Lena showing Paul the pictures in a book lying open on the table. In front of the table sits Madeleine, the eldest daughter, who, unmindful of the little wagon and doll by her side, is holding aloft the angel of the Christmas festival, in childlike ecstasy. There is, however, a shade of sadness on her happy face, upturned in the light of the tree to the little angel, as if she had some presentiment of soon becoming an angel herself. The third boy, in the midst of his sports, with his toy yet in his hand, has run to clasp his father's knee; whilst the youngest child has just come from its cradle, with its slip and night-cap, and bare feet, and nestling on the father's bosom, lovingly clasps him around the neck. This is the finishing touch to the picture, and reminds one of the description by one of our American poets, which could not be more real if it had been written for this Christmas scene:

> "An infant came from its cradle bed,
> And clung to the mother's breast;
> But soon to the knee of the sire it sped:
> *Love* was its gift, and the angels said
> That the baby's gift was best."

If now, to what meets the eye, we add music, — the Christmas hymn, and the children's hosanna, — the picture is perfect as a representation of a domestic Christmas eve. And this musical feature is suggested by the artist, in the instrument by Luther's side, leaning against his knee, as if he had just paused in some sweet melody and put down the lute for the caresses of the child and the fond endearment of the mother. It is truly a picture that touches the heart. It moreover brings into living view the great Reformer in the sweet, domestic enjoyment of Christmas, the happiest season of the year, and most exhilarating social festival of the Church.

Luther, in his teaching, restored to Christendom the true conception of the Christ-child, and the true meaning of the angels' song over the wonders of Bethlehem; and in his own experience and example, he has given the true ideal of Christmas in the family. This ideal of Christmas eve has mingled in the thoughts and songs and poetry of our finest literature.

We hear it in the recitative of Handel's divine strain: "There were shepherds abiding in the fields," as exquisite for truth and simplicity as the cheek of innocence. We know how Milton has sung of these angelic symphonies in the ode, "On the

Morning of Christ's Nativity;" and how Shakspeare has touched upon Christmas eve with a reverential tenderness sweet as if he had spoken it hushingly in a whisper.

> "*Some say* that ever 'gainst that season comes,
> Wherein our Saviour's birth is celebrate,
> *The bird of dawning* singeth all night long,
> And then, they say, no spirit dares stir abroad:
> The nights are wholesome; then no planets strike,
> No fairy takes, nor witch hath power to charm;
> *So hallow'd and so gracious* is the time."

Upon which, Horatio observes, in a sentence remarkable for the breadth and delicacy of its sentiment,

> "So have I heard, *and do in part believe it;*"

that is to say, he believed all that was worthy, and recognized the balmy and Christian impression produced upon well-disposed and sympathetic minds by reflection on the Christmas season.*

* Leigh Hunt: A Day by the Fire.

And so, as of old in Luther's home, let Christmas be hailed with a joyous welcome in all the families of Christendom. Let it be a Christian festival in the household as well as in the Church. Let it be a season for the warm outflow of all kindliness and love, and the sweet ministries of the heart- and home-life. Let every happy home be made happier by the Christmas-tree, with its fruit-laden branches dropping gifts into all hands. Christmas day brings a gift to all the world; for though in many a poor man's home there be no tree, yet where the tree is absent the cross stands present. Happy is he who, on Christmas day, abides within its sacred shadow, and receives the gift of gifts which God gave to the world in Him who is "the chief among ten thousand, and the one altogether lovely." Then let all unite in the joy and the song of earth and heaven:

> "Ring out, ye crystal spheres;
>   Once bless our human ears,
>   If ye have power to touch our senses so;
>   And let your silver chime
>   Move in melodious time,
>   And let the base of Heaven's deep organ blow,
>   And with your ninefold harmony
>   Make up full consort to the angelic symphony."

And then, in the genial warmth and sympathies of the season, let some tender heart-thoughts and kindly charities be given to the poor and homeless. For the return of every Christmas repeats the old German story of the poor and friendless outcast.

"On a certain Christmas eve, in a German city, while a Christmas-tree was sparkling in every house, a poor, homeless orphan was wandering, faint, weary, and cold, through the streets. He gazed longingly at the windows from which joyful lights streamed. He knocked timidly at door after door, but was unheeded. He would fain have gained entrance to one of those happy households, merely to look on, but no one heard him. At last he retired sick and miserable to a dark corner, and there, as he shivered with the cold of the December night, he remembered that an answer was promised to every sincere prayer. So he prayed to the Lord Jesus to give him a Christmas-tree. And as he prayed, he beheld a star in the distance; and as he gazed, the star approached him, and he descried the glorious form of a beautiful child. It was the Christ-child who came to answer his prayer, and who drew down stars from heaven to light a Christmas-tree for the poor orphan.

"And when the tree was all lighted, the Christ-child took the boy into the tree, and they were all wafted away into heaven. The next day the newspapers contained this item of city intelligence: 'Found in —— Street, the dead body of a boy, of some eight or ten years of age, parents unknown; coroner's verdict, death by starvation and cold.' The poor little outcast had left the world, outwardly in circumstances of extreme wretchedness, but inwardly in a dream of heaven, and in the arms of the Christ-child."

And so, with every return of Christmas eve, let the home be bright with the Christmas-tree, and glad with the music of children and the song of Bethlehem; and withal let the heart be tender and pitiful for the lonely outcast and neglected poor. And as through the cold, still night-air there comes echoing down the centuries the old, sweet, jubilant song of the angels over the cradle of the infant Saviour: "Glory to God in the highest, and on earth peace, good-will to man," let every heart be opened anew to the *holy child Jesus!* And let the young and the old, the home and the Church, yea, all Christendom unite to send back to heaven the song as angels brought it down: *Glory to God in the highest!*

> "Joy to the world, the Lord has come!
> Let earth receive her King:
> Let ev'ry heart prepare Him room,
> And heaven and nature sing."

. . . .

I

HOME IN SORROW.

HOME IN SORROW.

" 'T is sorrow builds the shining ladder up
  Whose golden rounds are our calamities,
  Whereon our firm feet planting, nearer God
  The spirit climbs, and hath its eyes unsealed."

NO portraiture of Luther's home-life would be true to nature and fact without those delicate shadings of sorrow which give to the picture its life-like completeness and heavenly sanctity. And hence, the artist, in his picture-life of the great Reformer, conducts us from the garden joys of summer, and the fireside pleasures of winter, to Luther kneeling by the coffin of Madeleine. The home but yesterday exhilarant with the music and festivities of Christmas is now overcast with shadows, and is sad and tearful in the silence of a great sorrow.

Luther found in his sad and early domestic experience that in his garden there was a sepulchre; and that the little coffin soon followed the Christmas-tree within his door. "Thy babe, O Bethlehem, turned in the sleep of that hallowed night his pure, pale face toward Gethsemane. The angel of the Christmas-tree could not guard the home from life's sorrows." More than in the summer-garden, or by the winter fireside, do we learn to know Luther, in all the tenderness of his nature and reach of his faith, in his home of sorrow and bereavement. It is then we see him as he appeared to Carlyle: "I know few things more touching than those soft breathings of affection, soft as a child's or a mother's, in this great wild heart of Luther. So honest, unadulterated with any cant; homely in their utterance; pure as water welling from the rock."

We pass from the sunny garden-scene to the shaded home, and from the hilarity and song of Christmas eve to the quiet vigils beside the couch of sickness, and to the deeper and sadder silence of death. It is but the picture of human life in its sudden alternations of joy and sorrow. For there is ever heard in the passing generations that plaintive sigh of the old bard on the banks of Ayr:

> "I've seen yon weary, winter sun,
> Twice forty times return,
> And ev'ry time has added proof
> That man was made to mourn."

In September, 1542, he was called from important Church interests, in Leipsic, to the bedside of his sick and dying child. One day, when she was in great suffering, he approached her bed, and taking hold of her little hands, covered them with kisses. "My dear child, my sweet, good Madeleine, I know you would like to remain with your father, but there is One still better in heaven waiting for you."

"Oh, yes, dear father," answered the dying child; "let the will of God be done."

The father continued, as he walked the room with deep emotion, "Dear child, oh, how I love her! 'The spirit is willing, but the flesh is weak.'" He opened the Bible, and read the passage in Isaiah: "Thy dead men shall live; together with my dead body shall they arise. Awake and sing, ye that dwell in dust, for thy dew is as the dew of herbs, and the earth shall cast out her dead." He then said, "My daughter, enter thou into thy resting-place in peace." She turned her eyes to him, with that last look of all mortal tenderness and immortal trust, and replied, with touching simplicity, "Yes, father."

The night before Madeleine's death, her mother, weary with watching, reclined her head on the sick-bed and slept, and dreamed. The next morning, as soon as Melancthon came, she told him her dream.

"I saw two young men, who seemed to be clad in robes of light, enter the room. I pointed to Madeleine, who lay in a quiet sleep, and made a sign to them not to disturb her; but they said they came to conduct her to the bridal ceremony."

Melancthon was very much affected by this dream, and afterwards said to his wife, "These were holy angels that Catharine saw, and were sent to carry the maiden to the true nuptials of a heavenly kingdom."

As the time of her departure drew near, she looked tenderly at her father and mother, and begged them not to weep for her. With a sweet smile upon her pale and dying countenance, she said, "I go to my Father in heaven." Luther, deeply moved, threw himself on his knees by her bedside, and, with clasped hands and bitter tears, prayed the Lord to spare her. Soon her consciousness ceased, and she breathed her last in the arms of her father. Catharine, in the agony of her sorrow, had turned away, unable to look upon her dying child. When all was over, Luther gently laid the head of his dear child upon the pillow, saying, "Dear Madeleine, thou hast found a Father in heaven! O my God, let thy will be done!" Melancthon, who, with his wife, was present, observed that the love of parents for their children is an image of the divine love impressed on the hearts of men. God does not love the beings he has created less than parents love their children.

The next day, Luther followed all that remained of his child to the grave; and as the coffin was lowered, he exclaimed: "Farewell, dear little Madeleine, farewell! but we shall meet again. Thou shalt rise again; shalt shine as the stars, yes, like the sun!" And then after a short pause, he continued: "I am joyful in spirit, but oh, how sad in the flesh! It is strange to know she is so happy in heaven, and yet to feel so sad!"

Then turning to the mother, who was weeping bitterly, he said: "Dear Catharine, remember where she is gone! she has made a blessed exchange! The heart bleeds; it is natural it should; but the spirit, the immortal spirit, rejoices. Happy are they who die young. Children do not doubt; they believe: with them all is trust, — they fall asleep in Jesus."

> "Some feelings are to mortals given
> With less of earth in them than heaven;

> And if there be a human tear
> From passion's dross refined and clear, —
> A tear so limpid and so meek
> It would not stain an angel's cheek, —
> 'T is that which Christian fathers shed
> Upon a pious daughter's head."

After the funeral, many friends came to express their sympathy with the bereaved parents. In answer to their words of condolence, Luther said: "I thank you, kind friends, for your sympathy; but do not grieve for me: I have given another angel to heaven. Oh, that we may each experience such a death; such a death I would gladly accept this moment."

To others, who addressed to him words of comfort, he said: "No, no; I am not sad: my dear angel is in heaven!"

Among the many compensatory and comforting thoughts of Luther under this great sorrow are those expressed in the following paragraph:

"The fate of our children, and above all, of girls, is ever a cause of uneasiness. I do not fear so much for boys; they can find a living anywhere, provided they know how to work. But it is different with girls. They, poor things, must search for employment staff in hand. A boy can enter the schools and attain eminence; but a girl cannot do much to advance herself, and is easily led away by bad example, and is lost. Therefore, without regret, I give up this dear one to our Lord. Children die without anguish; they know not the bitterness of death; it is as if they fell asleep."

Over the grave of Madeleine was placed a tombstone with her name, age, the day of her death, and a text of Scripture. Some time after, Luther composed a Latin inscription, which was carved on a monumental slab; and which breathes a spirit of subdued melancholy and resignation to God's will:

> "I, Luther's daughter Madeleine, with the saints here sleep,
> And, covered, calmly rest on this my couch of earth;
> Daughter of death I was, born of the seed of sin,
> But by Thy precious blood redeemed, O Christ, I live!" *

Soon after the burial, he wrote to his friend Justus Jonas: "You have no doubt heard of the birth of my Madeleine into the kingdom of Christ above. My wife and I ought to think only of praising God for her happy transition and peaceful end; for by it she has escaped the power of the flesh, the world, the Turks, and the devil. Yet nature is strong, and I cannot bear this event without tears and groans, or, to speak more truly, without a broken heart. On my very soul are engraved the looks, the words, the gestures of my obedient, my loving child during her life and on the bed of death. Even the death of Christ

---

* The Latin inscription is thus rendered in the "Conservative Reformation."

(and what are all deaths in comparison with that?) cannot tear her away from my thoughts, as it should. She was, as you know, so sweet and genial, so full of tenderness and love."

Luther never recovered fully from this affliction. It struck him to the heart. He looked upon it as an admonition of heaven; it was another thunderbolt. The first had taken from him Alexis, the friend of his youth; the second snatched from him an idolized child, the joy of his old age. From this time all his letters are tinged with melancholy: the raven wing of death was ever fluttering in his ear.[*]

On receiving a letter from the Elector, who wished him many years of a long life, he shook his head, and answered his royal friend: "The pitcher has gone too often to the well; it will break at last." One day,

[*] Audin's Life of Luther, page 486.

while preaching, he drew tears from his audience by announcing his approaching death: "The world is tired of me and I am tired of the world; soon shall we be divorced — the traveller will soon quit his lodging." *

The after-life of Luther was touched with a heavenly sadness. This affliction fell upon his home as the evening shadow falls, which at once hides the earth and unveils the sky. The serene and mellowing light of heaven sanctified the earthly home, as it now seemed nearer the heavenly. There was still a subdued and solemn joy in bereavement, as he thought of the two little ones of his household not unclothed but clothed upon. And he was happy in the assurance that they were now nurslings of heaven, and that soon he should meet them there;

* Audin.

"Forever and forever,
  Both in a happy home;
And there to stay a little while
  Till all the rest shall come."

This last phase of Luther's home-life has the pensive charm and beauty of sanctified sorrow. We see how Luther, when the hand of God touched him, kissed that chastening hand of his heavenly Father in meek submission and unmurmuring trust. That noble form, which neither kings, nor popes, nor devils could bend, is bowed in tears and sorrow by the sick-bed of his little child. The brave heart that never quailed before the thunders of Rome or the fires of martyrdom is broken and tender as an infant's beside the coffin of his little Madeleine. And yet, in all that tribulation and bereavement, there is not a word or a murmur against the ways of Providence. He is heart-sick and unspeakably sad, yet sweetly quiescent in the divine love; he is cast down and disquieted, but not in despair. And soon there is heard the old songs of faith and hope, "For God, our Maker, giveth songs in the night." And the song, like the nightingale's, is all the sweeter for the night. When all the instruments of human melody are broken, there is a hand that can touch the heart and waken the notes of melody and praise. And Luther felt the touches of that hand, and could exclaim with the Psalmist, "I will sing of mercy and judgment; unto thee, O Lord, will I sing." And so that home of the great Reformer, in bereavement, is a touching illustration of the Christian family in its sanctified sorrows and immortal hopes.

Sometimes sickness and sorrow will overcast our households with the shadow of death. Yes, afflictions will come to us all; the spoiler will desolate our happy homes;

but Jesus, who was so near and precious to Luther in his hour of trial, and poured the light of the resurrection morn into his weeping household, is our friend and Saviour; and will be with us with grace and sympathy, and with words of peace and unutterable consolation. And when our loved ones depart, we shall know that our Redeemer liveth, and that whosoever liveth and believeth in him shall never die:

> .... "And through the clouded glass
> Of our own bitter tears, we learn to look
> Undazzled on the kindness of God's face;
> Earth is too dark, and heaven alone shines through."

Let that home of Luther in Wittenberg, so beautiful in its summer joys and winter pleasures, and so sanctified in its sorrows of sickness and bereavement, be to us the true ideal type of the Christian family. Let our homes be Christian in form and spirit. Let the whole economy of the household be religious. Let the recreations and pleasures of home be sanctified by thoughts and hopes of the heavenly inheritance. Let every morning unite the household as at the gate of heaven, and every evening see it part with benediction as to its final rest. Then shall the sweet communions of the household be made immortal by hopes of heaven; and even the broken links in the family circle will be retained by Christian faith, and help to draw us heavenward.

God grant to each of us such a Christian home while we live; and when our time comes to depart, may our last look of earth be upon the faces we best love; may the gates that open into the heavenly city be from a Christian home. And knowing no better name for that world to which we go, we will look up with longing hope and tearful rapture and call it *Home.*

THE END.

www.ingramcontent.com/pod-product-compliance
Lightning Source LLC
Chambersburg PA
CBHW030317170426
43202CB00009B/1034